THE LAST ROUND

THE LAST ROUND

Randy Couture
with Sara Levin

HN Publishing

First published in paperback in November 2011
(Also in hardback as a limited edition)

Paperback ISBN: 978-0-9562586-6-3
Hardback ISBN: 978-09562586-7-0

Author: Randy Couture
Co-author: Sara Levin
Designer: Sara Levin
Cover Design: Martin Jennings and Sara Levin
Editor and Publisher: Fiaz Rafiq

Distributed by:

USA/CANADA
Midpoint Trade Books
27 West 20th Street, Suite 1102, NEW YORK NY 10011

UK
PGUK 8 The Arena,
Mollison Avenue, Enfield, LONDON EN3 7NJ

ACKNOWLEDGMENTS

This project could not have been complete without the trust and hospitality of Randy, Ryan and Annie (and Lou Dog) opening their home. Thanks is also due to the coaches, staff and members at Xtreme Couture MMA for welcoming me and my cameras without reserve. Thank you to Val Haney and Sam Spira, you make it all happen.

Thank you to Webster University, Dave Angel, Jon Cournoyer, Carol Hodson, Susan Stang, Jeff Hughes, Tom Lang, the art department staff and students for guidance and support in pursuing this book into fruition.

I will forever be grateful to USA Wrestling and the entire wrestling family. I would not be who I am today without the sport of wrestling in my life. Thank you to Art Martori, Jim Scherr, Ken Kraft, Pat Tocci and to all those who believed in me and fueled my passion in the sport.

Without the support and patience from my friends and family, I would be lost. It is impossible to list each of you, but you know who you are.

Thank you to my parents for their unconditional and unwavering love and support for every choice I have made on my life's path. There are no words for the admiration I have for you.

Randy, thank you for putting your faith in me and allowing me to be a part of your journey.

Follow your bliss.

- Sara

It's tough to thank every one who's contributed to my success over the course of my life. God has blessed me in so many ways, thanks goes to him for all that I am.

My mother deserves most of the credit for my character and work ethic. She has always been the rock on which I stand. I am closer with my father now than any time in my life. All I can say is, Dad, thanks for all you did.

To Sharan, Trish and Kim - things may not have worked out as planned, but thank you for the incalculable sacrifices you endured for the pursuit of my dreams and especially for the three wonderful children and two step children I've had the joy of seeing grow and develop.

To Ryan and Aimee, special thanks for all the countless hours spent in cars, planes and gyms around the world in support of your father. Ryan, you have no idea how proud I am to see the way you carry yourself in this sport we've chosen. Aimee, I'm so happy you've found a path that fulfills you.

I've had many coaches along the way, many of which were sorely needed male role models. Thanks to Coaches Casebeer, Macaboy, Seay, Burnett, Winter, Anderson, Chiapparelli and many others for all the time, encouragement and guidance. To all my teammates at Xtreme Couture, workout partners and opponents I've had the express pleasure to sweat and bleed with since the start. "Iron sharpens iron, just as one man sharpens another."

I have an amazing group of truly good people who've been there in support. Thanks to Scott and Val Haney, Sam Spira and Matt Walker. I don't know where I'd be without you all. Thanks to Zuffa, Frank and Lorenzo Fertitta, Dana White, and your amazing staff. We've had our rubs, but at the end of the day it comes down to a love for this sport. Thanks for the opportunity.

And last but not least, this project would not have happened if not for Sara Levin. Her creative intelligence and determination saw it through. You should be very proud. It's been a pleasure having you in my corner all these years.

- Randy

PREFACE

The sport of mixed martial arts (MMA) has come a long way since the first Ultimate Fighting Championship (UFC) took place in 1993 when Royce Gracie shocked the world when he beat bigger, stronger and heavier opponents. It wasn't until almost a decade and a half later when a more mainstream audience and media started to take serious note of this misunderstood sport which was branded "human cockfighting". The dedication and superior skills and technicality of the fighters, who trained as hard as any Olympic athlete, soon became apparent to the fastidious outsider.

The UFC broke pay-per-view records and arena attendance shot up around the country. On April 30, 2011, Randy Couture's final fight at UFC 129 in Toronto, Canada, broke the UFC arena attendance record with over 55,000 tickets sold. The sport of MMA has created global stars and champions in a short time it has been in existence. The popularity of the sport has been visible; it even overtook boxing in America. Live UFC events on Spike, and more recently the biggest TV network Fox, has further given the sport a wider mainstream exposure and the credibility of its athletes have been embraced.

Couture is an affable personality who has achieved more than most fighters in the game and is revered by MMA and world boxing champions. He is adulated by combat sports fans. Since the sport became accepted by a far more wider audience, a plethora of publications pertaining to the sport and its athletes hit the marketplace. As the demand grows and the fans are eager to find out more about their heroes and fighters, the top champions and fighters have garnered a fan base globally who endeavor to mesmerize their fans. Fans are an integral mix and play an imperative role in an athlete's success.

We are proud to present you a unique book which will be treasured by fans and enthusiasts alike. If you're a Randy Couture, MMA or combat sports fan, you won't be disappointed. If you want to know more about his life then you should take a look at his New York Times bestselling autobiography Becoming The Natural. This gifted athlete has now carved out an acting career in Hollywood, but the veneration he still receives from the fight fans is visible and will continue as he leaves a legacy which will endure for generations to come.

Editor/Publisher

"Couture
is ultimate fighting's
Babe Ruth.
His endurance, toughness
and proficiency embody
mixed martial arts."

- TIME

ABOUT THE AUTHORS

RANDY COUTURE

Randy Couture is the most decorated fighter in UFC history, with six separate title acquisitions over the span of fourteen years to his name. At 47 years old, Couture hung up his gloves on April 30, 2011, after his final fight with former light-heavyweight champion Lyoto Machida.

In 1997, at the age of 33, Couture made his UFC debut, defeating Tony Halme and Steven Graham in the heavyweight division. Couture then scored a TKO victory against Brazilian "Phenom" Vitor Belfort. After this fight Couture was given the nickname "The Natural". He earned his first heavyweight title fight in December 1997, after his match against kickboxer Maurice Smith. Couture TKO'd long-time number-one contender Chuck Liddell in his light-heavyweight debut. He became the only competitor to hold titles in both the heavyweight and light-heavyweight divisions of the UFC. This earned him his nickname "Captain America".

On June 24, 2006, Couture was the fourth fighter to be inducted into the UFC Hall of Fame, alongside Royce Gracie, Dan Severn and Ken Shamrock. At that point "The Natural" took a place in the UFC announcing booth and began pursuing a career in the motion picture industry. But watching Tim Sylvia's lackluster heavyweight title defense against Jeff Monson, Couture got the itch to get back in the Octagon. On March 3, 2007, he dominated Tim Sylvia, shutting him out on the scorecards. With this victory Couture became the first man to win the UFC heavyweight title three times.

Along with professional fighting, Couture has successfully authored three books - including his autobiography which was a New York Times bestseller - and is actively involved in numerous business ventures, while also pursuing an acting career. He partnered with Affliction to create the Xtreme Couture clothing line and expand the niche of clothing sponsorships for MMA athletes. He is also one of the founders of Round 5, the first company to create action figures for MMA athletes.

Couture's latest film was a leading role in Sylvester Stallone's The Expendables. The blockbuster movie featured an amazing cast including Sylvester Stallone, Jason Statham, Jet Li, Dolph Lundgren, Mickey Rourke and Eric Roberts to name a few. He also has a major role in the sequel, set to hit the big screen in the summer of 2012. He had a lead role in The Scorpion King II: Rise of a Warrior and has made appearances in movies which include Redbelt, Big Stan, Setup, Hijacked and Geezers, as well as the TV series The Unit.

Couture is involved in several business ventures which enjoy continuous success. His supplement line called Xtreme Couture Athletic Pharmaceuticals (XCAP) is taking off. Couture, along with Fox Sports' own Jay Glazer have started MMAthletics, a company which focuses on training professional athletes in different sports on the disciplines of MMA and how it can better them within their own sport. MMAthletics has worked with numerous NFL players: Matt Leinart, Patrick Willis, Jared Allen and Brian Cushing.

Couture currently resides in Las Vegas, NV, and is actively pursuing a successful acting career in Hollywood. He continues to train young professional and amateur MMA athletes at his gym Xtreme Couture. Couture's non-profit Xtreme Couture GI Foundation raises money and awareness for veterans wounded in action and their families. Although Couture is no longer active in the Octagon, he is very much involved in the MMA world and will go down in history as the man responsible for bringing the sport of MMA into the mainstream; one of the greatest champions and fighters in the world of combat sports.

Photo courtesy of Neal Burstyn/ntbcreative.com

SARA LEVIN

Randy and Sara began their friendship in 1998, when Randy was still training on the Greco-Roman national team and MMA was first breaking out. As a professional in the sports world and a fan of MMA, Levin has followed the evolution of the sport over the last 13 years and the contribution wrestling has made to its success. She has been an outspoken advocate for MMA and supporter of wrestlers in the sport as it has gained legitimacy.

Levin has a diverse background in sports marketing, graphic design and photography. She earned her bachelors degree in sport marketing and management from Indiana University. This launched Levin into a 10-year career in the Olympic Movement with USA Wrestling, the national governing body for amateur wrestling and the National Wrestling Hall of Fame and Museum. During her tenure at USA Wrestling, She was influential at the grassroots, national and international level of the sport. As national events manager she coordinated regional, national and international events including World Championships, Olympic Trials and the largest wrestling event in the world, the Junior Nationals in Fargo, North Dakota. She also served as marketing and promotions manager, directing the creative area of USA Wrestling, designing and producing the promotional materials for the organization and procuring and fulfilling sponsorship.

After a successful and gratifying career, Levin made the difficult decision to take her life in a new, artistic direction. In pursuit of a more creative career path and to expand her knowledge of photography and graphic design, She entered Webster University's masters program in studio art and completed her degree in 2011. She was one of three photographers with three images published in Kodachrome/The End of the Run: Photographs from the Final Batches. Her work has been shown at galleries and received awards from numerous juried exhibitions. Levin has been a frequent contributor to several well-respected wrestling photography websites.

Levin now lives in St. Louis, Missouri, where she continues her business as a freelance photographer and graphic designer.

INTRODUCTION

Welcome to The Last Round - a visual expose of the final steps in a life-long journey and passion in combative sports. So many people use the adversity of life as an excuse to fail. I look back and realize I could have been there, too. Instead, those challenges forged me into the person I am, who made a choice to achieve instead of being held back. For that adversity I am thankful.

Wrestling is the sport that started me on this path in high school. It was in the Army that I started to believe I could compete and win on the international level. That mindset and demeanor was honed to a fine edge at Oklahoma State University, where a long-standing tradition of wrestling excellence had been established.

Along comes a precarious introduction to a new combative sport, at that time called "no holds barred". A wrestler at Oregon State University pops in a VHS tape and up comes a former collegiate teammate, Don Frye brawling his way to victory! Immediately, I knew I had to try that! At first they said, "No thanks, we are looking for more exotic martial artists, you are just a wrestler."

The gauntlet had been tossed. I made it my mission to demonstrate what wrestlers were all about. The conditioning, intensity and technical mindset were paramount in wrestling, but more important to me was the purity and integrity represented in the world's oldest combative sport!

For me it wasn't about winning or losing. Trust me, I don't like to lose but I tried to keep it simple, be myself and do what I loved to do - compete! The fans seemed to appreciate my approach and stuck with me whether I won or lost. Even in this last round against Lyoto Machida, coming up short, the warmth, support and understanding from the fans was incredible!

I made the decision that I wanted to go out on my own terms, not after an injury or a couple of losses, when everyone is talking about how the sport has passed you by. That was important to me. I told family and few close friends. Everyone was very supportive and understanding. Sara Levin, a friend of 13 years and part of the "wrestling family" approached me with the idea of following me throughout this final phase in my competitive career. I wasn't keen on the idea at first. The thought of having someone in that close proximity for an extended period of time, even someone you know and like, did not appeal to me. My private life had already changed so much with the explosion of MMA that I didn't savor taking the invasion up another notch. After a lot of consideration, I knew this was a once in a lifetime opportunity. Thanks to Sara for making the process as painless as it could be. I hope you enjoy the fruits of our passion!

Randy Couture | Wrestling and MMA Champion and Actor

INTRODUCTION

I came to Randy with this project because I felt that the end of his competitive athletic career should not go undocumented. And he is too humble to think that his finale should be such a big deal. It took some effort to convince him that this was an important part of history and people would want to share it with him.

Randy has been a long-time friend and I have been one of his biggest fans since the day we met. This book was a chance to let others see what I have always seen in him. He possesses kindness and integrity like few people I have known. He has an honest laugh and humility in life. Here is someone who has been in the game since the beginning, and stayed very true to himself and his principle.

I was fully prepared to have my rose-colored glasses for Randy forcefully removed. I was ready to see sides of him I wouldn't like. But that never happened. What you see is what you get from him. He treats every person with respect and has a sense of loyalty like no one else. Randy's greatness comes from simplicity and honesty, it's magnetic and it is what makes him unlike anyone else.

This project was an opportunity to connect my photography and graphic design with a sport I love. More than just an MMA project, The Last Round is a visual exploration into the world of the combat sports athlete. The serendipitous nature of the Holga camera and the film process reflect the element of fortune that has pervaded Randy's journey into MMA and his continued success.

I chose to use the Holga, a plastic camera that uses 120 film - not something you see in sports very often. By utilizing the simplicity of this camera, it strips away the technology that permeates today's photography and focuses on the essence of the subject. To utilize a fixed focus camera means the photographer can't be a casual observer. In order to capture these images, I had to embed myself within the MMA environment, even entering the cage with two sparring fighters. I had to break the typical cloak of invisibility that a photographer tries to wear when shooting candid photography. The rudimentary technology forces a relationship with the subject that would have otherwise been unnecessary. The imperfections and unpredictable results of the photographic process capture the reality of Randy's journey towards his final round.

Just as individual combat sports like MMA and wrestling are raw and low-tech, so are the images in The Last Round. It is my intent that the candid style and intimacy of the photos will engage and connect the viewer. I hope that this book can be enjoyed as an essay on Randy's positive energy, intense drive and kind nature, as well as an artistic photographic compilation.

Sara Levin | Photographer, Designer, Fan and Friend

From the **start** of my career, from that first fight with Belfort, **nobody** gave me a snowball's chance in hell of **winning.**

"I didn't set out to be a fighter."

I had seen fighting and I was always intrigued by it as a sport. In a lot of ways I was already a fighter. I had been doing combative sports since I was 10 years old. But I didn't set out to be a fighter; I set out to show everybody what wrestling was all about, to represent wrestling.

Representing your sport was what it was all about in the early days of the UFC. It was all about "so-and-so was a Brazilian jiu-jitsu practitioner", or "such-and-such is the karate expert", or "that guy was a boxer". We were wrestlers.

This is how wrestlers operate, the conditioning, the intensity and competition we bring to the table is how we are as people, whether we win or lose. I quickly found that because of the legitimacy of the sport of wrestling, I automatically started shouldering the same burden as a fighter.

Although I came from the wrestling world, when I won a title in MMA people were looking at me not as a wrestler but as a mixed martial artist in a sport that was easily misunderstood by the media and public alike. Nobody knew what we were doing in wrestling and they were shocked to hear what we went through to compete. You would hear things like, "You cut weight? You spit in a cup? You wear plastics? How much weight did you lose? Oh, my God!" In MMA it was the same thing, "You get in a cage and you punch people? How do you do that?! You're friends with that guy? You guys are crazy!" It terrified people.

I was soon representing MMA the same way I intended to represent the sport of wrestling when I started out. I did it on a whim because it looked cool and I wanted to try it! I had no choice but to shoulder that responsibility. It was put on me; it came to me because of my success and background as a wrestler. Dan Severn was the first. Don Frye and Mark Coleman followed suit close behind. Then there was Kenny Monday and Kevin Jackson, who had achieved the highest accolades in wrestling as Olympic champions and then decided to try their hand at MMA. Again, this was something that was viewed as a fringe sport, and to gain legitimacy the validation had to come from the guys competing in it.

In the late 90s, Arizona Senator John McCain referred to the new sport as "human cockfighting" and led a crusade to ban it in all 50 states. He was a boxing fan and was horrified at the new, seemingly lawless sport. At the time the fights resembled no holds barred . . . but there were still three or four things that weren't allowed.

I will always love Zuffa's response to John McCain. They thanked him for hurtling the new sport into the political spotlight. It forced them to regulate the sport, make more rules and legitimize it. In the long run it really worked out for us.

February 28 - First day of training camp.
Xtreme Couture MMA; Las Vegas, NV

Things happen for a reason. Had I won my Olympic medal I probably wouldn't have been as hungry as I was at 34 to go into MMA and compete until I was 48.

When I'm training

everything else just goes **away.**

"I'm done, I'm gonna let this go."

Retiring from wrestling was definitely a conscious decision I made at the 2000 Olympic Trials in Dallas. There was no way I was going another four years. Making the Olympic team was the only thing I didn't achieve that I really wanted to in the sport. "I'm done, I'm gonna let this go," I said to myself. I decided to refocus and go back to fighting 100 percent. I was done juggling both. And by October that year, I was back in a title fight against Kevin Randleman at heavyweight.

Both wrestling and fighting are sports of experience. So much of what I knew from wrestling translated into an advantage in MMA. Wrestling gave me the leg up and carried me down the road, but at one point I felt like I had come to the end of the road.

At some levels I was frustrated with wrestling because I hadn't achieved my goals in it. Then losing to Garrett Lowney, a 19-year-old kid, who went on to win a medal I had been chasing for 16 years, really reinforced that it was over, it was done.

Up until my retirement in wrestling, I had been trying to do both wrestling and fighting. I had kind of been on the outs with the original parent company of the league, SEG, at that time over a contract dispute and the amount they were going to pay me. I had stepped away and was using MMA, predominantly jiu-jitsu, as a way of cross-training to stay in there and stay active. It was fun and I was learning a whole bunch of new stuff, but I wasn't really competing. I only competed a couple of times in a year and a half.

MMA was this whole new arena where not only was I going to continue to thrive as an athlete and learn new things, but also make a living. I could take care of my family and do the things I wanted to do as an adult. I could have easily made the decision to stay in wrestling another four years. I was certainly physically capable of competing. That still doesn't mean I would have made the 2004 team and won my medal.

I work harder to be in
better shape than my opponents.

I've pushed

myself in

ways I

never knew

I could.

Being a fighter has made

me a stronger person and

a more passionate athlete.

I felt like at some point
my body was
going to
let me
down.

Completing paperwork at the doctor's office.
Las Vegas, NV

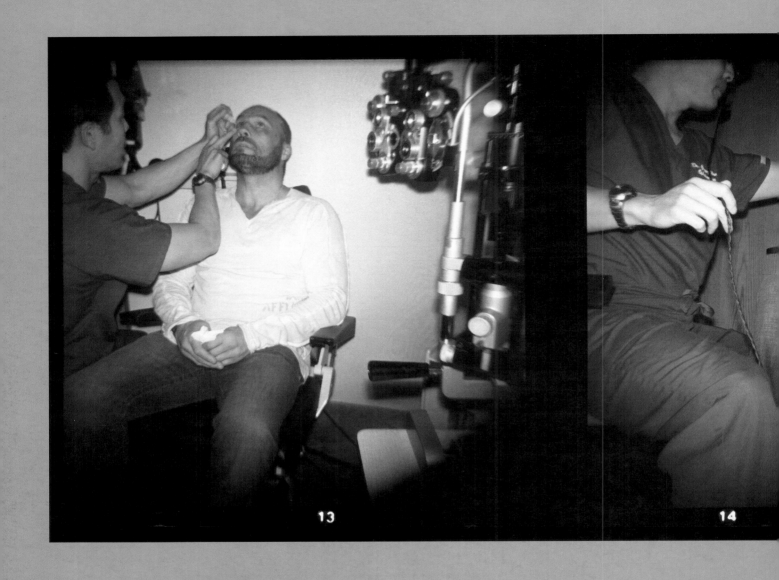

13

14

If the **worst** thing
that ever happens to me in
my life is to **lose**
a fight,

15   16

Annual eye exam for fighter certification.
Office of Dr. Gregory Hsu; Las Vegas, NV

then I'm doing pretty
            damn good.

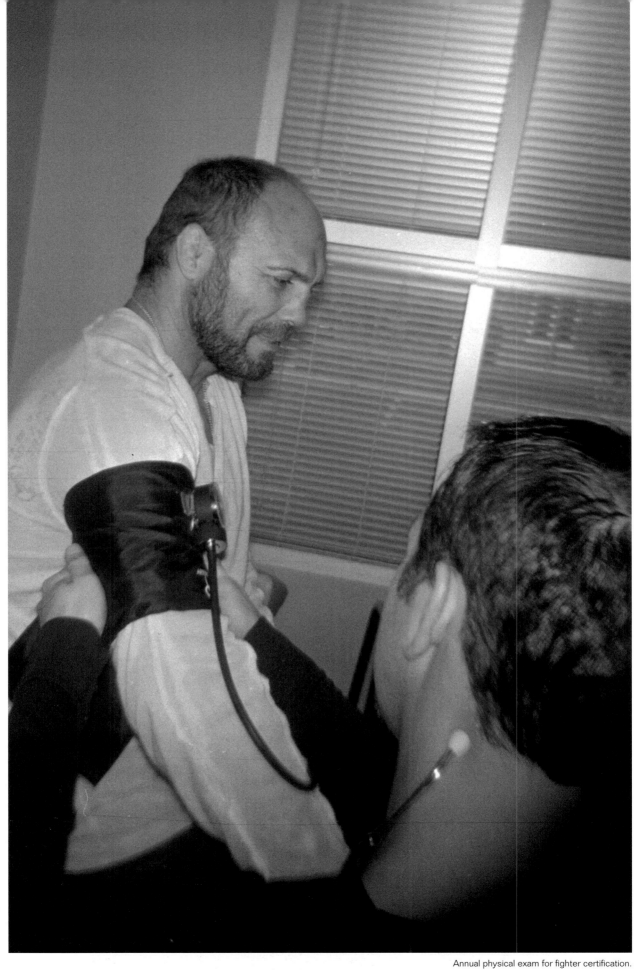

Annual physical exam for fighter certification.
Office of Dr. Randy Yee; Las Vegas, NV

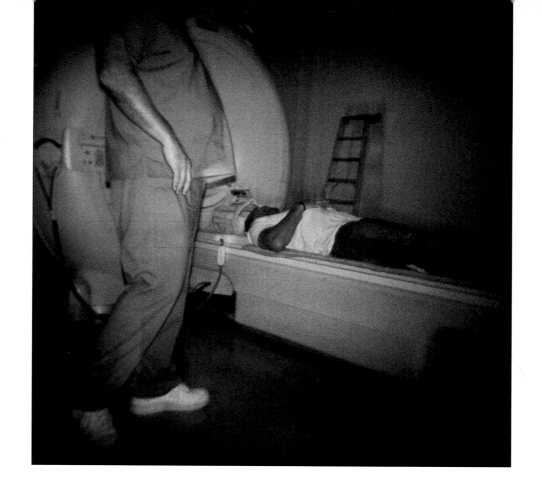

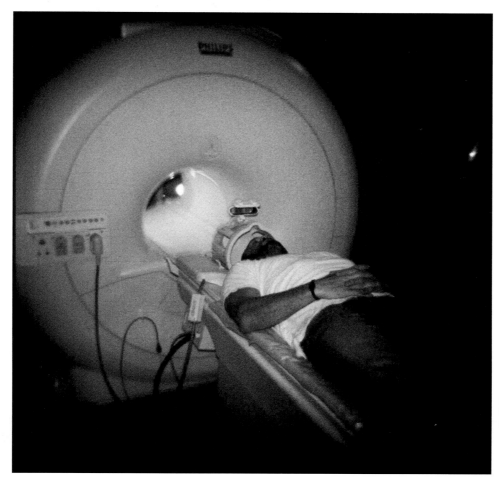

Annual MRI/CT scan for
fighter certification.
Las Vegas, NV

I was

just

doing it

the way

I thought

it

was

supposed

to be

done.

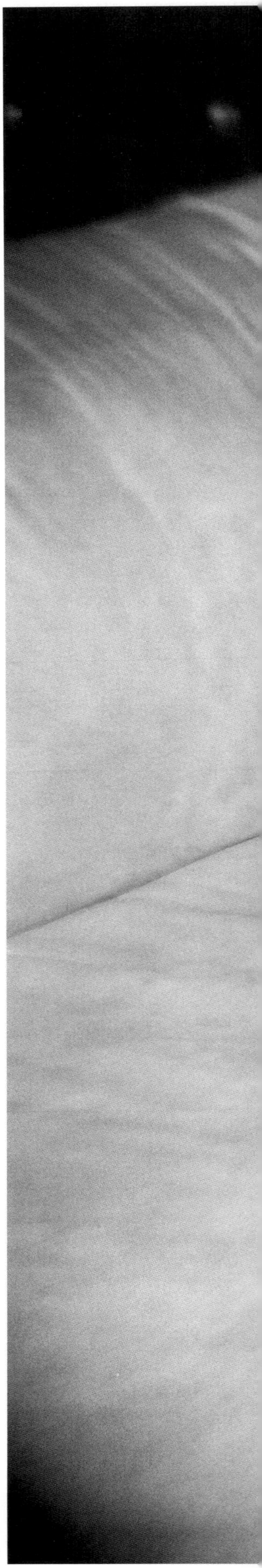

Relaxing at home.
Las Vegas, NV

Supplement shopping.
Whole Foods; Las Vegas, NV

Getting ready for morning workout.
Las Vegas, NV

I entered the sport on a whim

with no real expectations,

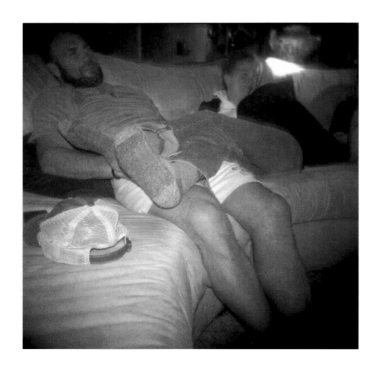 

so I have obviously far exceeded

any hopes I may have had.

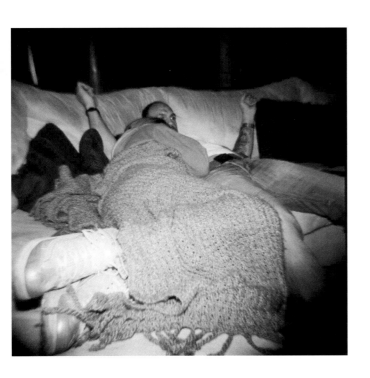

"It was surreal."

I didn't enter MMA to be famous or make money. I did it because I was intrigued and enamored by it and I wanted to try it. I perceived it just like wrestling. The icing on the cake was they were willing to give me a check to do it. That check happened to be bigger than any check anyone else had ever given me before.

I jumped into fighting on a whim; we wanted to show them what wrestlers were all about. It just looked like fun.

I had no idea who my opponents would be and wondered what the hell I'd gotten myself into at the weigh-ins in the lobby of the Holiday Inn in Augusta, Georgia, when 300lbs Tony Halme and 290lbs Steven Graham stepped on the scale as my competition for the title.

I fought twice in my first night, two huge guys. It was freaky. I had wrestled some heavyweight guys before. I trained with Matt Ghaffari all the time. I faced Tolly Thompson in a collegiate match. I had wrestled some big dudes and I knew you had to approach them differently, but it's a lot different in a fight. In a fight, someone's going to try to punch you in your face.

I still remember the first time walking out to fight and seeing that crazy crowd. That's just not something you get in wrestling. I mean, we have some big wrestling matches like Iowa and Oklahoma State or Oklahoma State and Penn State. Those were some big crowded, crazy fan events. But they didn't compare to walking out at that first fight. At the time, there were only 1,500 or 2,000 of those crazy fans. They were ripping at your clothes, hanging over the fence trying to touch you. Those four steps up into the cage, the sound of that cage door closing, the feel of that canvas under my feet, and the sensation of every hair on my body standing up at the same time! I wasn't sure if I wanted to piss myself and climb the fence to get out or stand and fight. I chose the latter and 50 seconds later I had my first victory by rear naked choke. It was surreal.

Dinner at home nine days before the fight.
Las Vegas, NV

At the office.
Xtreme Couture MMA; Las Vegas, NV

Reviewing contracts with lawyer/manager Sam Spira.
Las Vegas, NV

Office work with operations director Valerie Haney.
Xtreme Couture MMA; Las Vegas, NV

Photo shoot for the fight walkout shirt.
Xtreme Couture MMA; Las Vegas, NV

Hollywood is

calling now.

The acting bug

has bit me in

the ass **hard.**

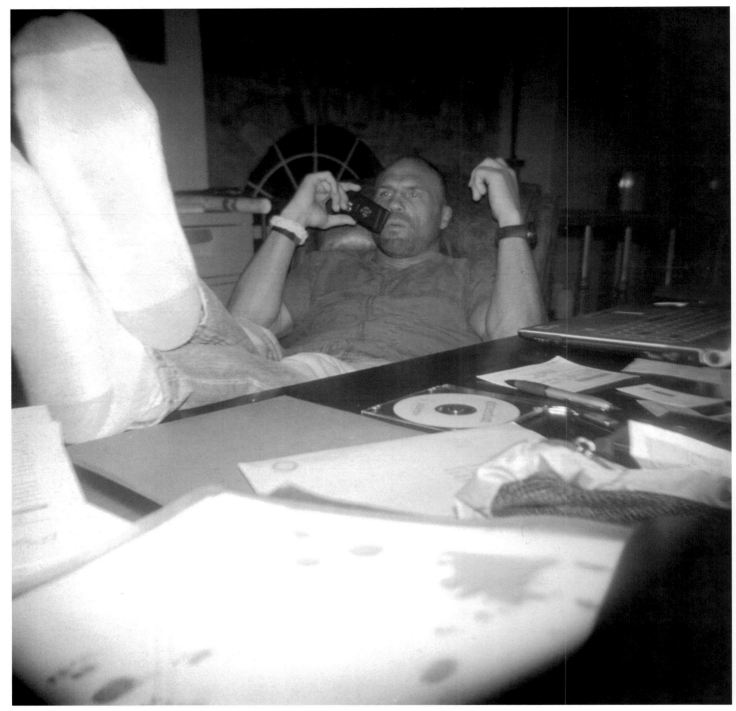

Phone interview with Australian press at home office.
Las Vegas, NV

Magazine interview at the gym.
Xtreme Couture MMA; Las Vegas, NV

Chatting with some fans at the gym.
Xtreme Couture MMA; Las Vegas, NV

Running into Cezar Ferreira, Vitor Belfort and son Davi at lunch.
Brio Tuscan Grille; Las Vegas, NV

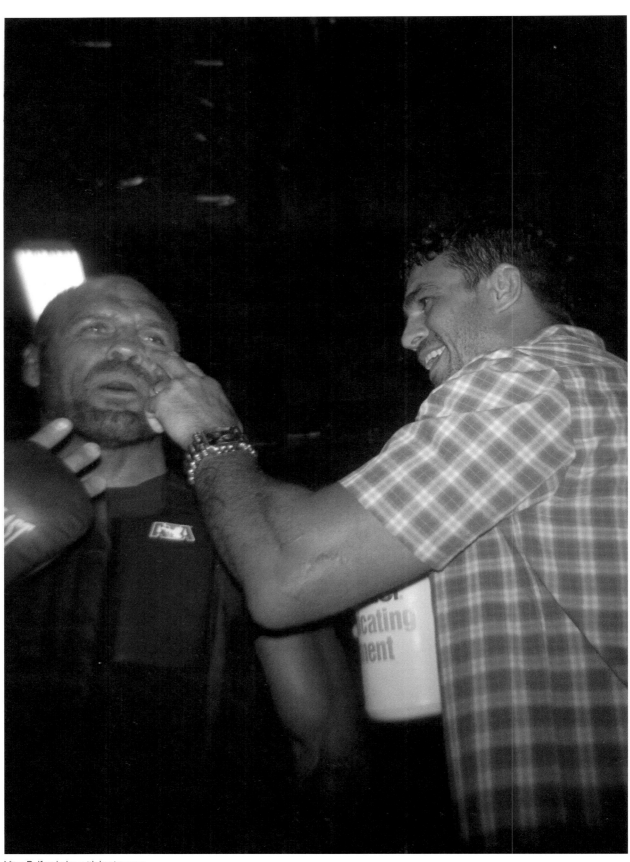

Vitor Belfort helps with boxing prep.
Xtreme Couture MMA; Las Vegas, NV

"Nobody expected me to win."

This whim just sort of took off, and the next thing I know is I'm fighting a superfight against Vitor Belfort, who had my full attention. He had fought on that same card I was first on, where he beat the hell out of Tank Abbott in 60 seconds. They said, "Well, we want you to fight this kid next in a superfight." I said, "Uh, OK." I immediately say to Rico, "We gotta get a boxing coach. This guy's hands are really good. He's fast, he's explosive." Again, looking at it from a wrestler's perspective, I'm thinking if I can tie this guy up and put him on the ground, I don't have to worry about that stuff. I'm not going to stand around and try to box with him. I think that fight set the tone for the rest of my career. Nobody thought I would win. Nobody knew who I was. Nobody expected me to win. And to go from that to fighting for the title . . . I was like, "Really?"

It's not like I had spent years at it. It wasn't like this was my career. This was just fun. It was a whole different mentality than what collegiate or Greco-Roman wrestling was for me at the time. This hadn't become a career for me yet. This was only my fourth fight and I had no idea what I was doing. I look at some of the old footage and the boxing technique I used in that fight against Belfort and it makes me laugh. I was so terrible at boxing! Then facing Mo Smith, a 17-year veteran of kickboxing, I realized that he knew as much about kickboxing as I knew about wrestling. Why would I want to stand around in front of this guy and let him kick me or punch me? No way. I'm gonna make this guy wrestle me. Every time he picks his foot up, I am taking him down. Back then everything for me was in wrestling terms. I didn't have a lot of other attributes. I was just starting to develop skills in some of those other areas.

The process of adding all these new techniques to my arsenal was fun for me. It was like turning a kid loose in a candy store, he doesn't know which jar he wants to run to first, which one he wants to sample or try. Comparing wrestling to that, wrestling for so long was about minor little adjustments. All those little nuances were what I had to focus on then. But in MMA every single day I learned a new technique, something big. I'm still learning. Even now after all these years I don't think I am ever done learning. There is just a vastness of technique, so many different guys and so many different styles. Think of the biggest candy store you've ever been in. Are you ever going to get into every jar in there for a taste of everything?

Sparring with training partner Cezar "Mutante" Ferreira.
Xtreme Couture MMA; Las Vegas, NV

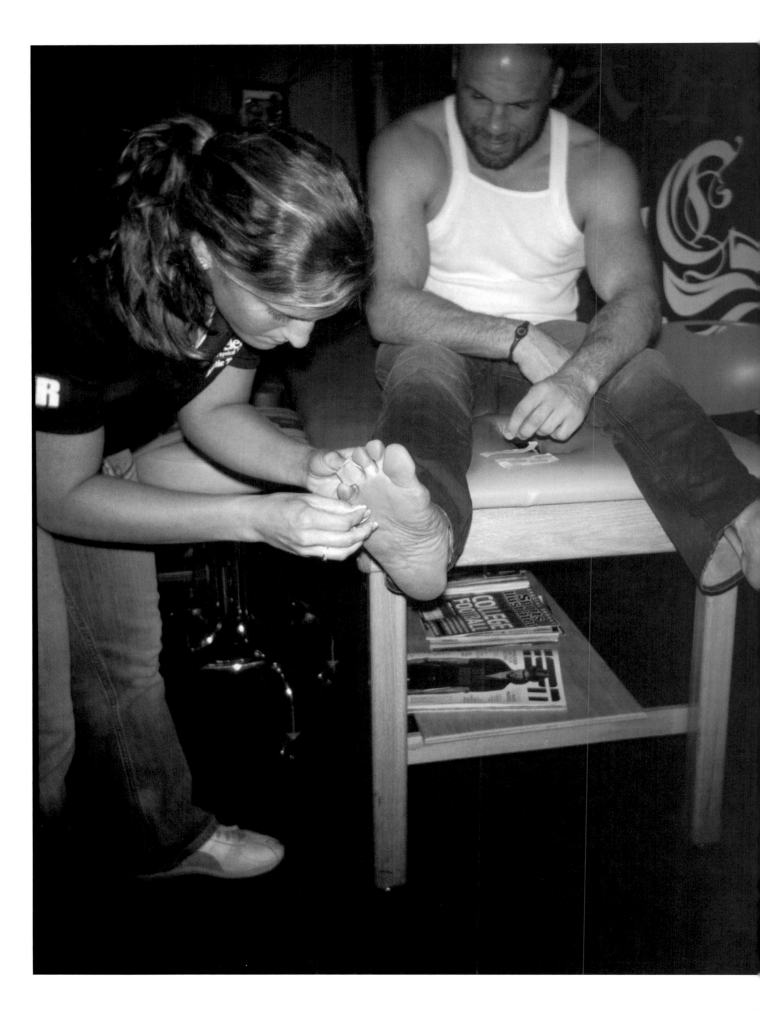

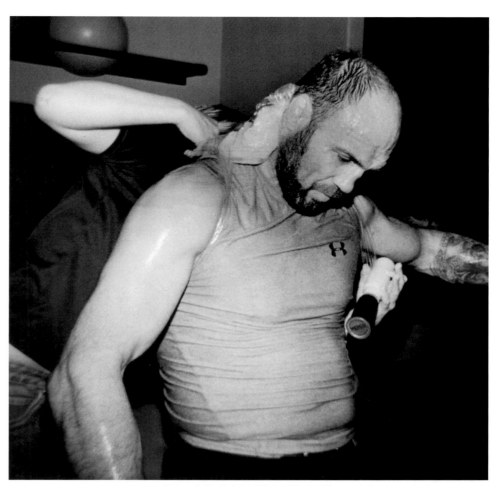

Trainer Caitlin Scheib of Select Physical Therapy helps secure ice to a sore neck.
Xtreme Couture MMA; Las Vegas, NV

An injured toe gets some aid from trainer Caitlin Scheib.
Xtreme Couture MMA; Las Vegas, NV

I was considered old when I started this.

Boxing practice with Coach Gil Martinez.
Xtreme Couture MMA; Las Vegas, NV

"It didn't matter if I won or lost, I was doing it because it was a freakin' blast!"

I learned a lot in that transition from wrestling to fighting. I realized that in wrestling I had seriously overtrained. I was forced to analyze psychologically why I felt so nervous before a wrestling match but I didn't get as anxious before a fight.

In wrestling I was putting all this pressure on myself to win. Every single match held the weight of whether I made the team or failed again. I was all cued up for every single wrestling match. I was smiling and laughing when I was fighting, I wasn't nervous at all.

It wasn't that I didn't care; the pressure was just so different for fighting. With wrestling the goals I set gave me a fear of failure and I had failed a couple of times. I lost both the NCAA finals and the Olympic Trials finals twice. I had failures in fighting, too, but in that transition time moving from one to the other, I was able to analyze my anxieties.

I think it really solidified my decision by staying true to why I was fighting. It didn't matter if I won or lost, I was doing it because it's a freakin' blast! I love it, it's fun and all the rest of that stuff doesn't matter.

You train as hard as you can, you learn what you need to learn, you sharpen the tools you need to sharpen for each given opponent because they each pose different problems. I think that if I had learned those lessons earlier in wrestling I probably would have made the Olympic team and won a medal.

In wrestling I had become overtrained and flat. I think part of that was that my coaches didn't know the difference. As Americans, we have the mentality of "harder, harder, harder, beat them up, go until we make them quit" instead of learning to train smarter. The Russians and the Cubans weren't busting their butts three days out from the weigh-ins. They were doing light one-hour workouts. We thought, "Geez, must be nice." They were in recovery mode; it made sense, they had already done the hard work. The hay was in the barn. They were going into a tournament and looking stellar and amazing, while we were scrapping for every little thing we could get. The coaching staff hadn't figured out yet how to peak for a competition. I was their bright example of a work ethic of being there on time, showing up early, staying and doing extra work. I was the guy they pointed to and I took pride in that. Really, it just compounded the problem.

Throughout my MMA career, though, I seemed to thrive more and shine more when I wasn't expected to win. The times when I was the champ and everyone was gunning for me was much harder to deal with than being the underdog. Because I was already older, generally I was always the underdog. I seemed to flourish in the underdog spot. Those were the times when I stepped up. I had confidence in my training plan and confidence in my ability to win those fights and that is what came through. I know it was much more difficult for me when I was expected to win, expected to perform - that's just me.

Conditioning with Coach Jake Bonacci.
Xtreme Couture MMA; Las Vegas, NV

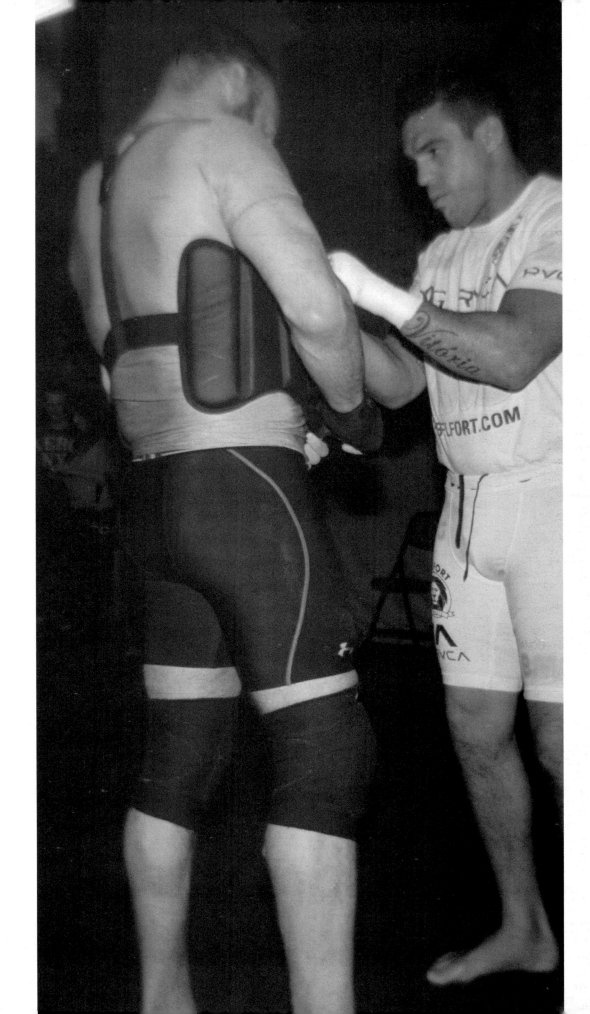

April 21 - Last hard practice, talking strategies with boxing Coach Gil Martinez.
Xtreme Couture MMA; Las Vegas, NV

April 21 - Grappling Coach Neil Melanson making notes on fight strategy.
Xtreme Couture MMA; Las Vegas, NV

You may walk out there by yourself, but you are **definitely** not alone.

April 21 - Randy's fight team discusses fight week's game plan.
Xtreme Couture MMA; Las Vegas, NV

The last time I retired I felt
like I was doing it for all
the **wrong** reasons.

This time, it's for the
right reasons.

April 21 - Last hard practice of camp.
Xtreme Couture MMA; Las Vegas, NV

April 28 - Workout at Xtreme Couture MMA Toronto.
Toronto, CAN

"You're only as good as your last fight."

Week in and week out on any given day you are either the stud in the line up or you're getting your ass beat. In the wrestling world, about the time you start thinking you are "all that" someone comes along and cleans your clock. It's the same in the MMA world. One slip, one mistake, the smallest little thing can cost you a fight.

The public is really difficult to please. With a lot of people, you are only as good as your last fight. I'm cognizant about this and I take a lot of it in stride. I don't get emotional or fired up over it. I know it's not the end of the world to lose a fight and I think having that attitude keeps me on track. Nobody likes to lose, it's not like I enjoy it, but if the worst thing that ever happens to me in my life is to lose a fight then I'm doing pretty damn good.

Resilience is just something you learn from wrestling. I have had some of the biggest matches you can have in this country and I have been on both ends of them. Whether you win or lose, the guys you trained with and your family are still there. That special bond and support keeps you going.

Wrestling is a lifestyle that you grow up into. Your dad did it, your uncles did it, your best friend's brother did it and that's why you do it. It just becomes a part of your life and culture; it isn't about trying to escape anything. Unlike a lot of other combat sports like karate or boxing, wrestling isn't a vehicle to get out of a situation. In a lot of ways, that is why wrestling is still so pure, it isn't a vehicle to anywhere! You wrestle simply because you love it.

That has changed a bit because of MMA. I think now wrestling can be a vehicle into professional athletics because of MMA, but that wasn't always the case. Wrestlers have a different set of eyes, a different approach. They experience things in a different way. I think wrestling translates well to MMA because there are a ton of similarities that wrestlers can take advantage of.

When I walk out into the center of that wrestling mat, it's just my opponent and me. If I jump into that cage, it's the same thing, just me and the other guy. There's something about that individual combative sport. All the things you train yourself to do and put yourself through to get ready to go out there and perform, to carry the weight of all that adversity and stand out there by yourself shapes you. It builds a particular character.

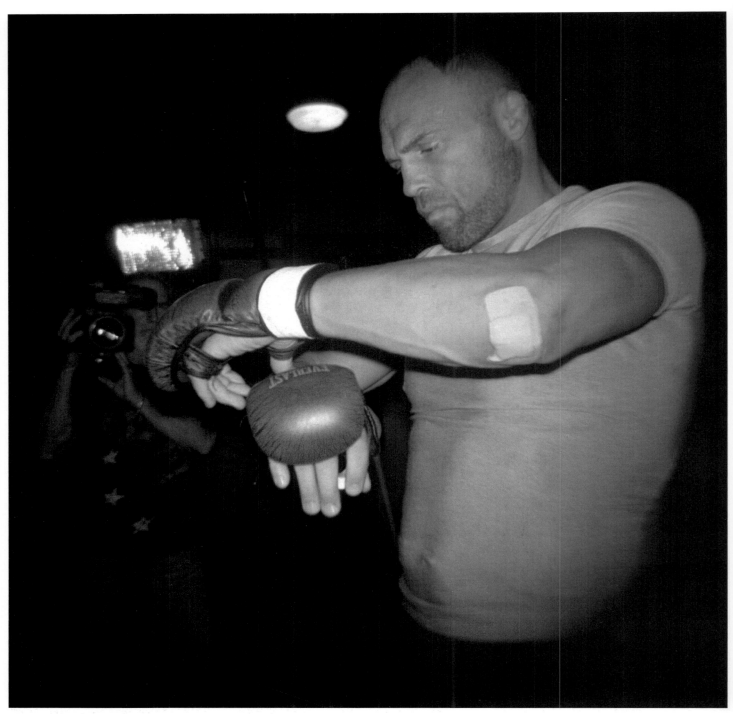

Putting on the gloves for light practice.
Xtreme Couture MMA Toronto; Toronto, CAN

Television interview two days before fight.
Xtreme Couture MMA Toronto; Toronto, CAN

MMA H.E.A.T.'s Karyn Bryant provides Portuguese interpreting for training partner Cezar Ferreira.
Xtreme Couture MMA Toronto; Toronto, CAN

It's emotional,
no doubt. Win or lose,
this is definitely
my **last** fight.
I want to go out
on my own terms,
in my own way,
with a fight
I choose.

Walking to dinner with mother, Sharan and sister Traci.
Toronto, CAN

Walking from dinner with sister Traci.
Toronto, CAN

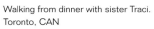

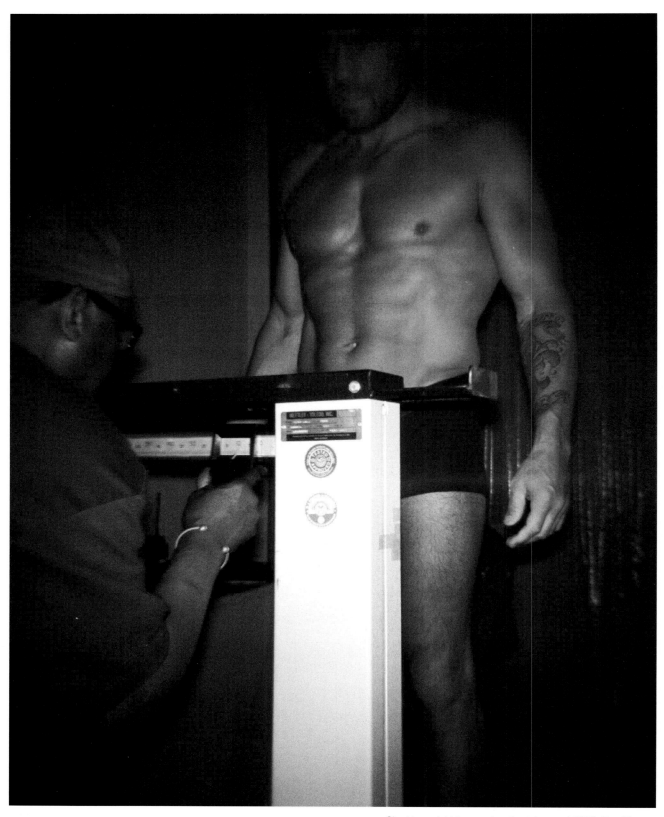

Checking weight the morning of weigh-ins with UFC's Burt Watson.
Westin Harbour Castle; Toronto, CAN

"I set forth a goal and achieved it."

Wrestling is the sport that started me on this path. From that first headlock and bloody nose, to setting the goal of winning a state championship and seeing it through, I found technical and physical challenges that pushed me to be the best I could be.

In 1981, I had been working a job as a box boy at the farmers market where my mom worked in the meat department. I needed the job because I had to pay for my own car insurance and gas, which was part of the deal of me having a car.

Well, I decided that I wanted to focus my senior year on wrestling because I felt I could win the state championships. So, I talked to my mom and my boss, told them I needed to dedicate a lot of extra time to achieving this goal. My mom agreed to support me and my boss said it was great. So I quit my job and my mom helped me out with the insurance and gas so I could keep my car.

I did the running and other extra things I needed to do. I ended up winning the state title that year. I was the first state champion in any sport for my high school. That was the first time that I had ever really sat down, planned and mapped out where I wanted to go and what I needed to do to get there. I set forth a goal and achieved it. That ultimately shaped the athlete and ultimately the type of person that I am today.

I still have that bracket, the regional and state brackets, framed and warped in my mom's garage.

I've been competing my whole life in something.

I'll figure out something to compete in,

even if it's foosball

Cutting weight at the hotel fitness center.
Westin Harbour Castle; Toronto, CAN

— probably **contact** foosball.

On weight, lined up and ready for weigh-ins.
Ricoh Centre; Toronto, CAN

Randy and Jay Glazer waiting for weigh-ins behind Lyoto Machida and Steven Seagal.
Ricoh Centre; Toronto, CAN

Randy and Lyoto Machida waiting to weigh-in.
Ricoh Centre; Toronto, CAN

Weigh-ins are like a poker game -
guys have tells and sometimes fights
are won
or lost in
that moment
on stage.

April 29 - The final weigh-in.
Ricoh Centre, Toronto, CAN

Dinner after weigh-ins at hotel restaurant.
Westin Harbour Castle; Toronto, CAN

"Look, who are you gonna be?!"

Coaching is something that I always feel good about, have an affinity for and enjoy. I have that coaching bone that came from wrestling and I have a unique opportunity to share the benefit of my experiences. I enjoyed my time coaching at Oregon State and at Centennial High School. The level of competition never mattered, I like the mentoring aspect of athletics.

I think if Joe Wells, the head wrestling coach at Oregon State University, had let me stay on I probably would have stayed there and continued to juggle both fighting and coaching. Joe forced me to make a choice. He gave me an ultimatum. He said, "Look, what are you gonna be? Are you gonna be a fighter or a coach?" And I told him I was going to fight. I had to make a decision. I've never really had the opportunity to thank him. I was kind of angry at first to be forced to make that choice. Ultimately, after a couple years with things turning out the way they did, I was happy with the decision. I look back and I'm glad he forced me to make that choice. I would have tried to do both.

I could always go back to wrestling and I've always felt like I could fall back on it. I could get back into the college ranks or do more fore wrestling in high schools or even just the club we have here in Las Vegas. But I don't really know if that is where I will end up, I think I will end up doing something in MMA, maybe as a commentator.

It's not that I look at wrestling as a step back. I will always be a wrestler. I will always love wrestling. There is just more prospects in MMA and I've spent the last 13 years of my life with this sport, so I really see more of an opportunity to flourish and make a living in it, to continue to support the people I care about. Wrestling is still not a terribly lucrative sport; it's a sport of passion for sure.

MMA changes all the time, but administrative opportunities are still there for me. I have realistically been acting in movies for seven years now; it's not like I am a flash in the pan. I have been paying dues, working my way up and it's been a long time coming. There may come a time when I have to choose, but I'm hoping I can continue to juggle both those balls at the same time.

Randy and old friends Phil Lanzatella, Kenny Popelka, Tony Demos, Jesse Moorehead, Doug House and Mark Edwards.
Westin Harbour Castle; Toronto, CAN

Fight week is like homecoming to me, it's an excuse to

get the guys together from the various phases in my life.

April 30 - Relaxing on fight
day in the hotel with Annie.
Westin Harbour Castle; Toronto, CAN

Team Couture on fight day in the hotel room.
Westin Harbour Castle; Toronto, CAN

Leaving for the fight.
Westin Harbour Castle; Toronto, CAN

"The time is right to close this chapter."

With my decision to retire for good becoming public, I actually feel more comfortable with it. I know it's the right decision. I'm more confident with it, more settled with it. In an ESPN interview, Franklin McNeil asked me about the Fedor fight and whether or not I was going to keep the door open to come back and fight Fedor in Strikeforce if they offered it. I was quick to answer no. I'm done, I'm in a different place in my life and I think he is, too. I closed the door on that a long time ago.

I'm in such a different place now than the first time I retired. After that third Chuck Liddell fight I was feeling so crappy. I was walking around at 200 pounds and I didn't even have to cut weight. There was so much stress between the divorce, my businesses and my mom. It was a crazy time. I just didn't feel like myself. I needed a break. I needed to step out and do something else.

Things settled down about six months later and I started to feel like myself again. I did a submission grappling tournament in California and had so much fun training for it. Just being at a competitive event rekindled the fire.

You still might find me entering a grappling tournament again just to stay active. But the rational side of me is saying the time is right to close this chapter, the terms are good. I am happy, I am healthy and I have all these other projects going on. I feel terrific! I have to pinch myself because of how good things are going right now. I don't know what I'd do if I felt any better! I am really excited about the prospects in my future, exploring a theatrical career. I don't want to stay until I feel bad again and retire a third time, or suffer another injury or loss. I don't want to be that guy.

I honestly feel that I can retire from fighting without having missed out on anything. I can't think of a single thing more that I could wish for. I've experienced everything you can experience in this sport. If you talk about styles or fights, I never got that one punch knockout. It was the only thing that never happened in a fight. The Tim Silvia fight was the closest I came to experiencing the one-punch knockout. But that's never been my style.

I've had it all. It's all happened.

Packed in the hotel elevator leaving for the fight.
Westin Harbour Castle; Toronto, CAN

Getting a first look at the record setting 55,000 people in attendance at the stadium, with Jay Glazer, Cezar Ferreira, Neil Melanson, Ryan Couture and Sam Spira.
Rogers Centre; Toronto, CAN

Checking out the stadium and greeting fans.
Rogers Centre; Toronto, CAN

Chuck Liddell stops
in the locker room.
Rogers Centre; Toronto, CAN

It's been said that I'm too nice
and nice guys finish last.

Well, I'm proof that doesn't hold water.

UFC's Greg Hendrick with some parting words.
Rogers Centre; Toronto, CAN

Prewalk with Team Couture - Ryan Couture, Neil Melanson, Jay Glazer and Cezar Ferreira.
Rogers Centre; Toronto, CAN

Randy and team in the locker room - Cezar Ferreira, Ryan Couture, Hiroshi Allen, Jay Glazer, Neil Melanson.
Rogers Centre; Toronto, CAN

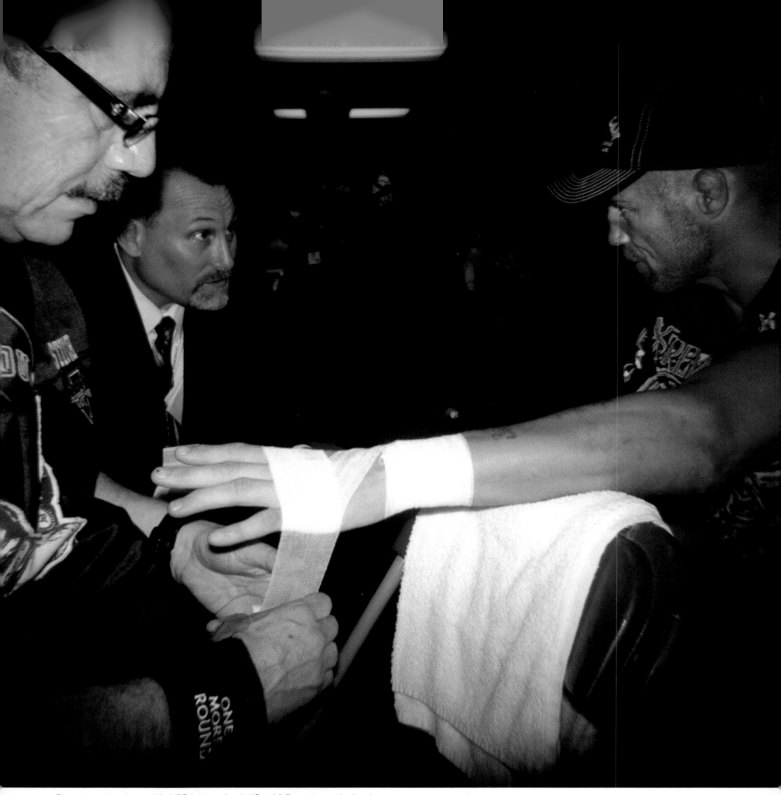

Receiving instructions while UFC cutman Jacob "Stitch" Duran tapes the hands.
Rogers Centre; Toronto, CAN

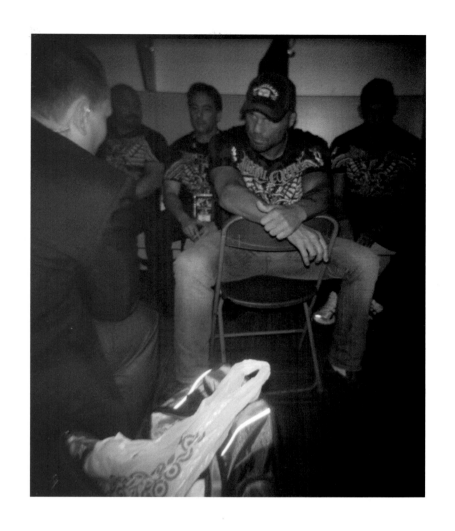

Visualization is a huge part of preparation.

Getting my hands taped is one of the first triggers

that puts me in the frame of mind to go do battle.

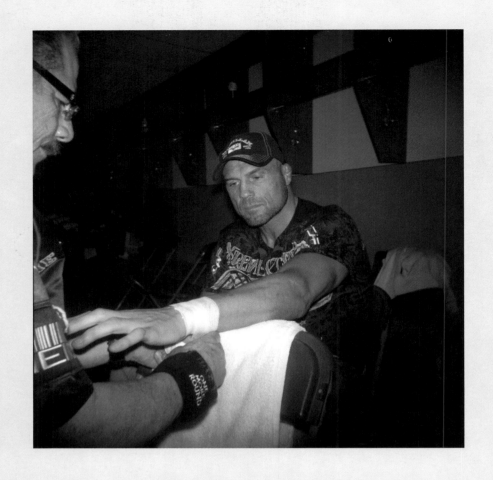

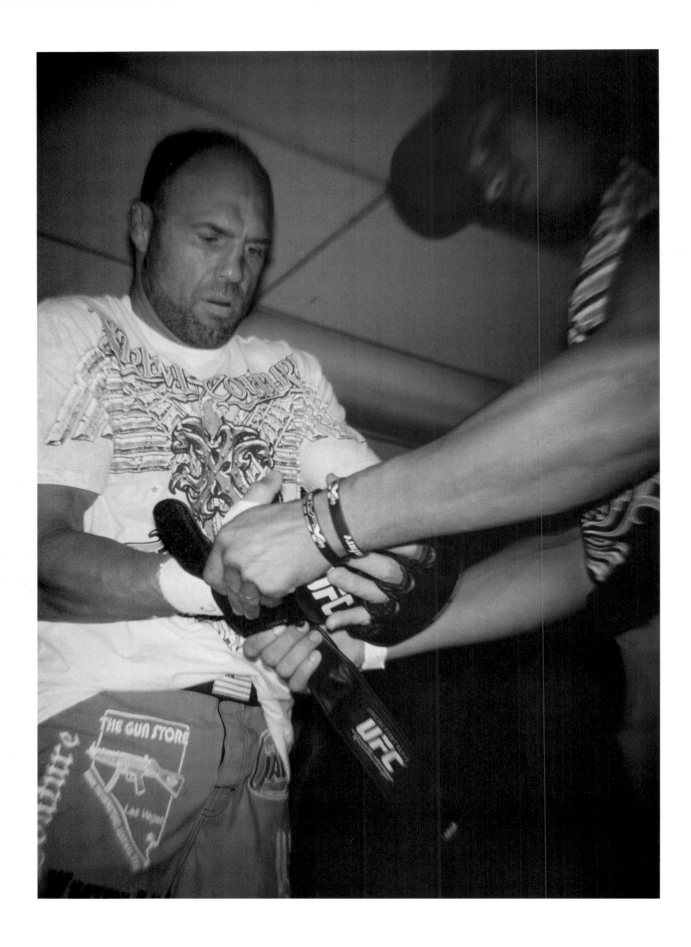

"Pay attention or get run over."

I'm able to compartmentalize my life because I can focus well. Competing and working out is my way of focusing and it has always been a stress reliever to me. If you can't focus in that moment, then you've got issues, something going on.

One of the reasons I like riding a motorcycle so much is you have to be in the moment and you can't go on autopilot. You have to pay attention or you'll get run over, and there is something very freeing about that.

When I was a kid and in trouble or stressed out, I would take my dirt bike over to the field across from the school and just spin donuts. It was a stress reliever. That's how training is now. I go into the gym and there's no room for anything else in my mind. I have to be right there, in the moment and physical. Fighting is the same way. Wrestling is the same way. All the other stuff just goes away when I am training.

I have a lot of other stuff going on and a lot of other things pulling at me, but nothing needs my immediate attention. Nothing is so crucial that it can't sit for a week or a month. Those things aren't going anywhere, they aren't going to change and they are nothing I can solve immediately.

On the other hand, the gym doesn't come home with me. I don't like to talk about fighting when I get together with my real friends, and they don't try to make me. That's how I know I am with my normal inner circle of friends. Other people want to talk about fighting, ask questions and discuss technique. That's not what I want to do with my free time.

My life experiences, being what they were, have made me a master juggler, constantly having to keep so many balls in the air: service, life, kids, wife, college, wrestling, international wrestling, coaching . . . I am constantly juggling all these things and shifting focus as they need to be dealt with. The only way to do that is to compartmentalize and focus on what is in front of me right now.

Father and son in the locker room.
Rogers Centre; Toronto, CAN

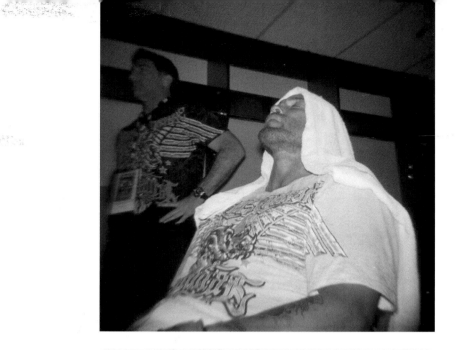

Moments before the last walkout.
Rogers Centre; Toronto, CAN

Fans lining the walkout path.
Rogers Centre; Toronto, CAN

"I'm proud of the whole thing – from start to finish."

I do think the UFC would look very different if I hadn't been a part of it. Everything would have been different had I made the team instead of Garrett Lowney . . .

I think I have certainly affected how people fight from a technical perspective. I wasn't the only guy doing it but I definitely perfected "dirty boxing" and the "ground and pound" styles. I took a very cerebral approach to my fights; I figured out the strengths and weaknesses of an opponent and tried to exploit those things. I am not the only fighter who did that, but there have been several examples where that has been highlighted in some big fights in my career.

From a public perspective, I think I affected how the sport is viewed, I had a hand in getting it widely accepted. People had to push aside their misconceptions and first impressions and take a second look at it. I am relatable, I could just as easily be the guy living next door to you, you wouldn't think twice about it or be taken aback. I'd like to say that maybe I could date your daughter and you wouldn't have a problem with it, but that's probably not true.

As far as my career, I'm proud of the whole thing - from start to finish. I'm just as proud of the way I handled the times that I lost or didn't come out on top and the times that I won and proved everybody wrong. I tried to react the same either way. I wanted to be the type of person who is just as gracious when I won titles as when I lost titles. That's the one thing people fail to recognize . . . yeah, I won the title six times, but that means I lost it just as many.

To do what I've done I had to face a lot of adversity. I've lost a lot but I kept going, picked myself up, made some changes and came back to win it again. That's what it's all about.

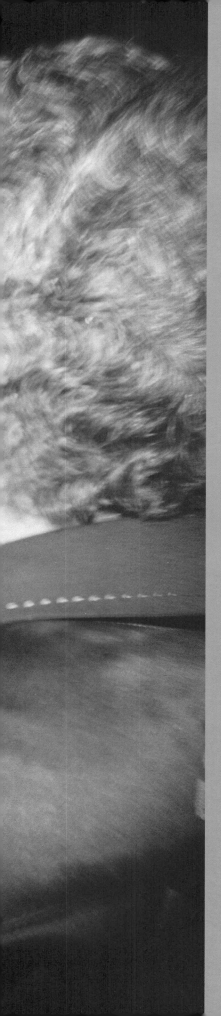

This is the last one.

The final step into the Octagon.
Rogers Centre; Toronto, CAN

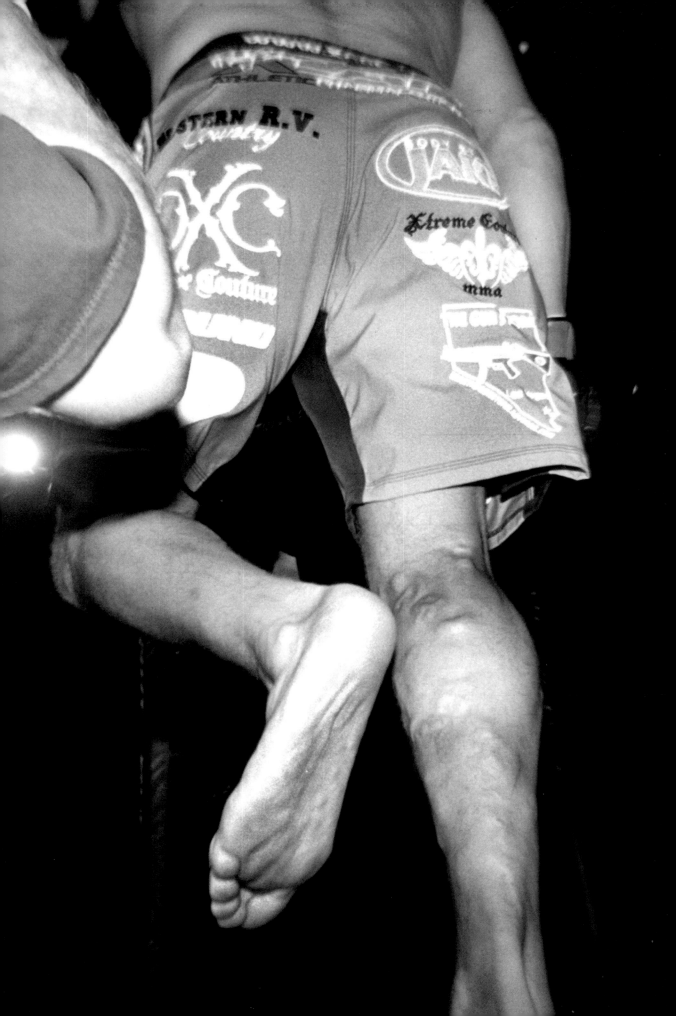

"I did what I love to do, compete."

As much as I like the void of living simply to compete - eating, sleeping and training - I feel like I am coming to a stage in my life where I want all these other things more. I want to go out and enjoy my life. I want to ride my motorcycle on the weekend. I want to make another movie. As much fun as it is to compete, at some point enough is enough.

I don't want to wait until I injure my neck so seriously that it bothers me for the rest of my life. My other joints could give out and my knees are pretty stiff compared to what they used to be. I used to be able to sit with my heels under me and lay all the way back to touch my head on the mat. I can't do that anymore. Even doing the normal walkover step for a shot where you touch your knee on the mat hurts. I'm just not as flexible as I used to be.

Thankfully, I adapted my wrestling technique to fit fighting and I don't have to get as low as I would in a wrestling match. I have all the skills and tools still functioning to win a fight and to compete at the same level. My body hasn't betrayed me yet, but I don't want to keep fighting until it does.

I'm not sad about ending my career, I have been wrestling since I was 10. There's a lot of different ways to compete in life. I don't feel sad about this being the last one because I feel fulfilled. Even with wrestling, win or lose, I don't take for granted anything I learned along the way.

I entered the sport on a whim with no real expectations, so I have certainly surpassed any hopes I started with. To fight for a title belt in my fourth competition is pretty crazy, and certainly unexpected. Also, having the sport explode the way it did has been a different ride with a whole other different set of expectations. It was amazing to achieve things individually, but to also see the sport take off the way it has and become so popular is fantastic. It wasn't like that in the beginning, I didn't get into it for the fame and I'd still be doing if it wasn't popular.

Yeah . . . I know they're going to throw more opportunities at me. There's a lot of chatter about me facing Jon Jones, but it's tough to see that actually happening. When Zuffa bought Strikeforce, there was chatter I could go over to fight Fedor, which a lot of people have wanted to see for a long time. That's a fight I've always been interested in. But then I start feeling my neck and the stupidest little things that set it off. I'm just trying to be rational and realistic about where I'm at and what I really want to focus on.

I came to terms with the Fedor fight years ago when I spent 13 months chasing it and I let it go back then. I'm sticking to my guns - this is my last fight. I'm making great money and my retirement home in Colorado is almost done. I have other business ventures and they are doing well. I don't think there's any reason to continue to beat myself up. To be honest, the competition is done.

Of course, having those unachieved goals will always linger in my mind. Being an NCAA champion would make me part of a very rare group of guys. I was there twice and didn't get the job done and that's frustrating, but I'm proud of everything I've accomplished in MMA. I have been on top six times, even being one of the oldest guys in the cage, in two different weight classes.

I did what I love to do, compete. I don't think there's anything in MMA that I didn't achieve that I wanted to. I can't honestly say that about wrestling. There were things that I didn't get done but those lessons came through in fighting. It all worked out the way it was supposed to work out.

Leaving the arena after the fight.
Rogers Centre, Toronto, CAN

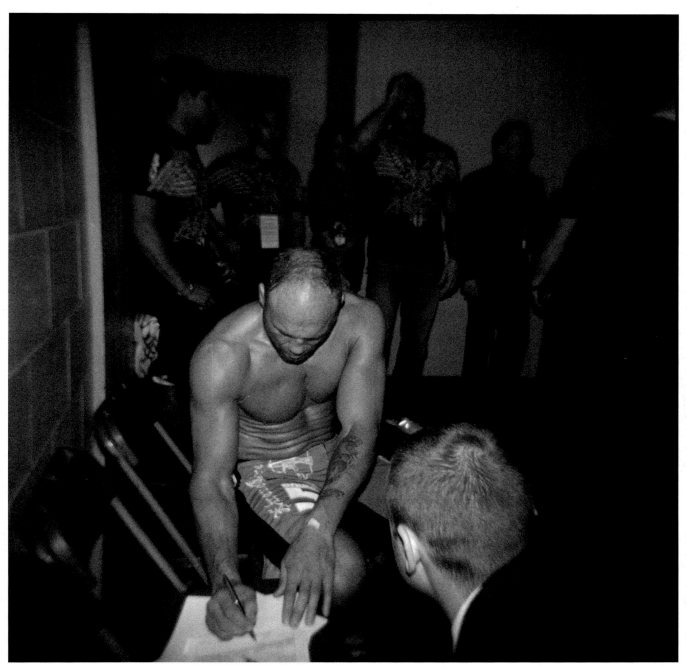

Signing paperwork after the fight.
Rogers Centre; Toronto, CAN

Tooth in hand in the locker room after the knockout.
Rogers Centre; Toronto, CAN

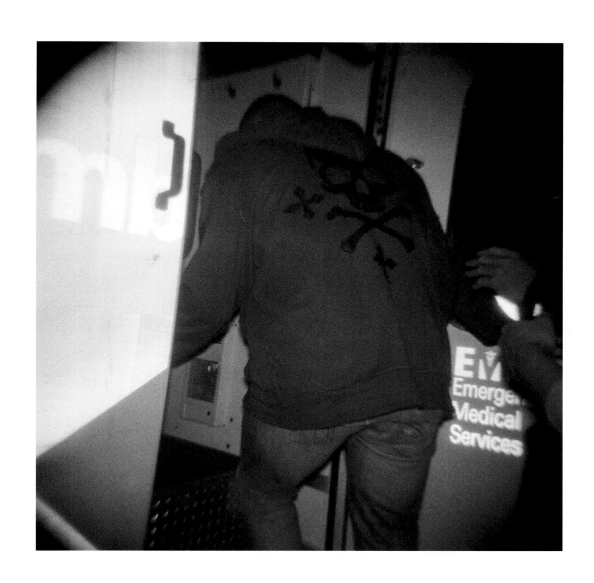

"I am absolutely content. Not many people can say that."

I have been an integral part of this sport as well as a witness to its maturity. I think all of us as athletes started this by laying down the groundwork and jumping over the hurdles that were put in front of us to legitimize it. If something were to change at this stage in the game and another hurdle presented itself, I think any one of us would step up.

I've never felt like I owed anything to the sport. I was just doing what I love to do. As an athlete, you have a passion that you want to be accepted and it's hard to have what you are striving for be so misunderstood. Everyone thought we were crazy, dangerous criminals. We aren't. That's something I am willing to fight for and represent.

There have certainly been times when I've felt like I was giving more to the sport than I got in return. That's a difficult thing to delineate. On the other hand, I have made a tremendous living over the past 14 years in this sport. I've made more money than I've ever made in my entire life, or probably would have made, as a professional athlete in this sport. For that, my family is taken care of and I am very, very comfortable.

In a lot of ways it's been a pretty even give and take. I've rode this thing, been involved in representing it and making it a legitimate, respected and understandable sport and I think I have done that with integrity. In return I have made a good living and had an absolute blast along the way. It's been good. I don't feel cheated. I don't feel uneven. I am absolutely content. Not many people can say that.

IT'S NOT THE END; IT'S A NEW BEGINNING

Randy Couture is able to resonate with fans and public alike beyond the confines of the MMA arena and the world of combat sports. After he became widely acknowledged as the greatest UFC and MMA fighter, responsible for bringing the sport of MMA into the mainstream, Couture was able to parlay himself from the Octagon into Hollywood. His role in Sylvester Stallone's The Expendables further catapulted him into a whole new world, this elevated his profile like no other MMA fighter. After playing several parts in a number of noted movies, Couture has become a prominent athlete-turned-actor who continues to pursue and work on projects in Hollywood alongside prominent and elite stars in the movie industry.

Making movies is an enjoyable experience for this revered former UFC champion, working alongside the likes of Jason Statham, Sylvester Stallone, Bruce Willis and 50 Cent to name a few. Whilst fighting in the Octagon, Couture became a fan favorite and the most popular and influential fighter. His fan base rocketed when he made the transition to acting. When MMA fans will look back at the sport in decades to come, Couture will always be perceived and acknowledged as being a pioneer in the sport's history. For Couture, retiring from the arena is not the end; it's the new beginning of another career. There's no doubt we will be seeing him on the big screen for a long time alongside some of the biggest action stars in Hollywood.

Couture has made an impact and influenced many people and personalities. When promoting The Expendables, Stallone told talk show host David Letterman, "Randy kept air-mailing people. We shot in an old fort with solid brick walls, and I would notice these stuntmen hitting the walls. And finally they were begging me, 'Don't let him touch me. I can't take it. I'm so beat up I can't breathe.' Steve Austin is a big guy but he was going, 'Please, take me out.'" Stallone who himself influenced millions of people with his tough-guy persona with the Rocky and Rambo franchises continued, "Someone asked me, 'You put all these tough guys, Dolph Lundgren, Jet Li, in a room together, who comes out?' If you walked in 10 minutes later you'd see Randy Couture sitting on top of us having a chocolate fudge sundae."

For decades fighters have come and gone in the combat sports world. Some become world champions and then fade away into obscurity; others make an indelible impact on the sport and capture the hearts and minds of the people and go down in the history books. Moreover, some elite athletes are blessed and pursue further careers which keeps them in the limelight even after their retirement. Randy Couture will always be remembered as one of the godfathers of MMA. This is not the end; it's just the starting of a new beginning . . .

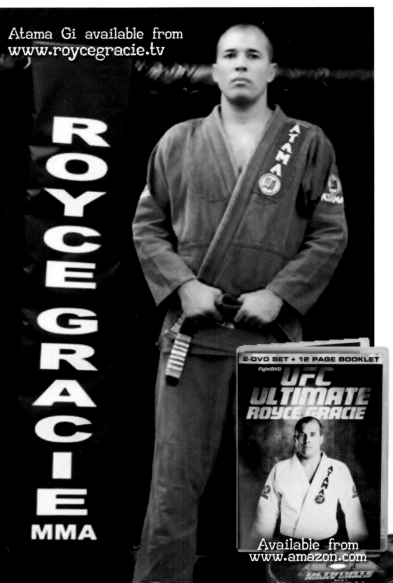
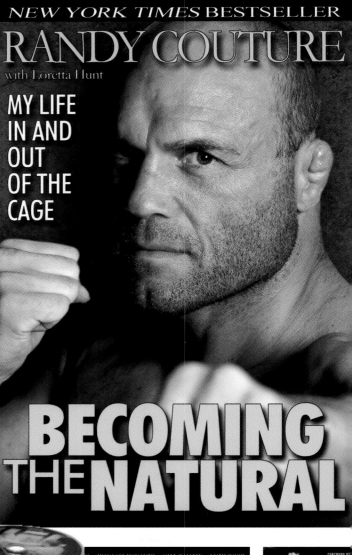

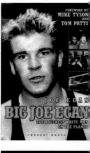